Unraveling the Mysteries of AWS Glue Timeout Errors

Table of Contents

Chapter 1. Introduction

As we embark on an enlightening cruise through the labyrinth known as AWS Glue, we're set to demystify one of the most notorious issues that professionals often grapple with—Timeout errors. This Special Report, titled "Unraveling the Mysteries of AWS Glue Timeout Errors," aims to guide users through the intricate pathways of cloud computing and Big Data processing solutions, making the complex, quickly graspable. Whether you are an experienced data engineer trying to troubleshoot that nagging problem, or a novice seeking to broaden your field of knowledge, this report strikes a balance between detailed accuracy and accessible clarity. We'll drill down together into the layers of AWS Glue, transforming what might initially seem daunting into an opportunity for learning and growth. Our journey promises to be more than just instructive—it's essential preparation for your next data processing endeavor. Dive in to untangle the knotty puzzles of timeout errors, and emerge empowered. Let's decode the indecipherable!

Chapter 2. The Origins of AWS Glue and Timeout Errors

To comprehend the complex layers of AWS Glue and the timeout errors associated with it, we must first delve into its origins. AWS Glue is a fully managed extract, transform, and load (ETL) service that helps create, run, and monitor data integration pipelines with ease. A branch of the Amazon Web Services (AWS) offerings, AWS Glue hinges on the central premise: minimizing the unduly time-consuming and challenging data preparation steps for analytics.

In a world that's fast becoming data-dependent, it is no surprise that this service's introduction in 2016, at the AWS re:Invent conference, was welcomed with open arms by the data handling community. The appeal of AWS Glue lies in its unification of several data preparation tasks under one umbrella, thus serving as a one-stop-shop solution.

2.1. The Case of Timeout Errors

For all of AWS Glue's charm, there exists a bogeyman that confounds many—timeout errors. These malefactors, primarily timeouts on JDBC and Python shell jobs, can truly test your problem-solving mettle. Understanding the root of this perplexity involves a look into what constitutes a timeout error in AWS Glue.

A timeout error typically occurs when a data processing job exceeds the allocated job duration, causing the operation to abruptly terminate. In AWS Glue, the default limit for a single job run is 48 hours. If a job runs beyond this time frame without being completed, the system interrupts the job, resulting in a dreaded timeout error.

The propensity of such errors depends on an array of factors, such as the size and nature of the dataset, the complexity of the data transformation operations, and the efficiency of the code written. Timeout errors are not just annoying; they disrupt critical work, waste resources, and could cost companies both time and money.

2.2. The Part Played by Data and Jobs

Appreciating the intricacies of AWS Glue timeout errors requires a basic understanding of how data and jobs play their part in this cloud-based ETL service. In AWS Glue, data is stored in 'tables,' much like how one would store data in a relational database. These tables can be part of 'databases,' which act like containers for the tables. The data for these tables can be sourced from a variety of sources such as Amazon S3 buckets or JDBC databases, among others.

Jobs in AWS Glue are the heart of data operations. Be it extracting, transforming, or loading—everything is performed by these jobs. They can be written in Python or Scala and allow for flexible data transformation. Each job has a time limit, which, when exceeded, gives birth to our main antagonist—timeout errors.

2.3. The Intertwining of Data Catalog, Crawlers, and Timeout Errors

Another critical player in our understanding of timeout errors is the AWS Glue Data Catalog. This catalog is your go-to metadata repository, customizable, searchable, and filled to the brim with metadata tables ready for your AWS Glue and Amazon Athena applications.

The Data Catalog simplifies and accelerates analysis by allowing you to create and manage a unified metadata repository across various services, consolidate metadata exploration and metadata management, and simplify metadata crawling. From here comes another pertinent role player—the crawler.

The AWS Glue crawler connects to your source or target data store, progresses through a prioritized list of classifiers to determine the schema for your data, and then creates metadata tables in the AWS Glue Data Catalog. However, at times, these crawlers might still be executing even after the allocated time lapses, leading to the occurrence of timeout errors.

2.4. The Ensuing Impact and This Journey Forward

In this intricate labyrinth of AWS Glue, timeout errors, seemingly trivial, rise as potential impediments to seamless data operations. The complexity compounds when working on large datasets or executing extensive transformation operations where jobs tend to overrun their allocated time. Now that we acknowledge the origin and the troublesome potential of this issue, we stand better prepared to mitigate its impact.

Steer through the following chapters as we take you deeper into the realms of AWS Glue, shedding light on the anatomy of timeout errors, and how to troubleshoot them. This meticulous exploration promises to equip you with advanced methodologies, concrete code solutions, and strategic practices to tame timeout errors in AWS Glue effectively. Just like any labyrinth, the way out of AWS Glue's complexities gets clearer as we navigate together, unmasking the unknown and making the path less hazy for future endeavors.

Chapter 3. Understanding AWS Glue: An Overview

AWS Glue, as part of Amazon Web Services, is a fully managed extract, transform, and load (ETL) service that allows users to move data between data stores. It has increasingly become an indispensable tool in the field of cloud computing and Big Data processing, mainly due to its serverless nature, scalability, and integration with a wide range of AWS services.

3.1. What is AWS Glue?

In essence, AWS Glue is an ETL service that automates the time-consuming steps of data preparation for analytics. It categorizes your data, cleans it, enriches it, and moves it reliably between various data stores. Glue automatically generates the code to execute your data transformations and data loading processes.

It's equally important to note that AWS Glue is serverless, which means that you don't need to manage any infrastructure to use it. It scales spontaneously, processing your data as quickly as possible. With AWS Glue, costly up-front provisioning is a thing of the past, as you pay only for the resources you consume while your jobs are running.

3.2. AWS Glue Components

AWS Glue consists of a central metadata repository known as the AWS Glue Data Catalog, an ETL engine that automatically generates Python or Scala code, and a flexible scheduler that handles dependency resolution, job monitoring, and retries. AWS Glue is integrated with a wide array of AWS services, allowing you to create ETL jobs that interact with these services.

Let's look at some of the primary components of AWS Glue:

1. **Data Catalog:** The Data Catalog is a service central to AWS Glue. It's like a pre-built database repository where metadata related to data sources, transformations, and targets is stored. The Data Catalog maintains a unified view of your data, which is vital for ETL jobs and making sense out of complex data networks.

2. **ETL Engine:** This element produces Python or Scala code (depending on the user's preference) that extracts data from its source, transforms it, and loads it into a specified data store. The beauty of this ETL Engine is its ease of use—you don't need to be an expert coder as Glue auto-generates the necessary code.

3. **Scheduler:** This module manages job orchestration, dependency resolution, job execution, error handling, and recovery. It's also possible to set triggers in the Scheduler for ETL jobs to start or stop based on conditions you specify.

3.3. AWS Glue Features

Key characteristics make AWS Glue an appealing choice for ETL processes:

1. **Automation:** The automatic generation of ETL code by AWS Glue expedites the process of setting up ETL jobs. It even suggests transformations, saving significant development time.

2. **Serverless:** As a serverless service, AWS Glue eliminates the need for server allocation or management. Users pay only for the resources used while the ETL jobs are running.

3. **Data Catalog:** As mentioned earlier, the Data Catalog provides consistent metadata storage, making it easy to manage data across large databases and warehouses.

4. **Developer Endpoint:** AWS Glue allows developers to write their ETL code with increased accuracy and sophistication by enabling

them to create a development endpoint and to connect their favorite IDE with the Glue ETL engine.

3.4. Working with AWS Glue

Before commencing, make sure that you have an active AWS account. AWS Glue requires an Amazon S3 bucket for storing your ETL job artifacts and scripts. It integrates with Amazon S3, Amazon RDS, Amazon Redshift, and other AWS services effortlessly, allowing you to centrally manage, control, and audit your data-processing routines.

The general process for managing ETL process using AWS Glue generally involves:

1. Cataloging your data by pointing AWS Glue to data stored in Amazon S3 or other supported data stores.

2. Generating and modifying an ETL script. AWS Glue will recover a sample of your data and suggest transformations, after which you can modify the script to meet your specific requirements.

3. Running your ETL job. Simply schedule when you would like your job to commence, AWS Glue handles resource provisioning, task orchestration, error handling, etc.

4. Checking the statistics associated with your ETL job.

3.5. Behind the Scenes of AWS Glue

Under the hood, the operation of AWS Glue revolves around three core actions—crawl, process and load.

- **Crawl:** In this first phase, AWS Glue connects to your source or target data store(s), progresses through a chosen data subset, and extracts metadata. It then catalogues this metadata for future reference during ETL jobs.

- **Process:** AWS Glue does the heavy lifting during the processing stage. Based on anticipated or specified redundancies, inconsistencies, or required changes, it runs transformations on your data in its ETL environment.

- **Load:** Finally, once the data has been processed to your specifications, AWS Glue loads it into the target data store(s). As part of loading, you can choose to either overwrite existing data or append the new data.

By piecing together these puzzles, we can appreciate how AWS Glue functions and how it has come to be an integral part of data management in the AWS ecosystem. With a grasp of these fundamentals, we can now embark on overcoming one of the common stumbling blocks - the notorious timeout errors. As we sail through, remember that with technology, every challenge is an opportunity for knowledge enhancement. Let's decode the indecipherable!

Chapter 4. Delving into Data and Networking Architectures

To begin our journey into the heart of AWS Glue, we must commence with an understanding of the backbone structures that facilitate the transfer and manipulation of data – the data and networking architectures.

The well-planned union of these two domains, namely data architecture and networking architecture, is the lifeblood of any data processing and computing service, AWS Glue notwithstanding. In such a system, data architecture frames the foundation, offering a schematic representation of information, while networking architecture provides the physical support, linking various computing resources together via network infrastructure.

4.1. Understanding Data Architecture

Data architecture defines data sources, its organization, administration, and guidelines for data manipulation. AWS Glue plays a pivotal part, allowing for the automated discovery of data, viewing of associated metadata, and generation of ETL jobs to traverse data barriers.

The data catalog, data stores, and ETL jobs are three primary components of Glue's data architecture. The data catalog offers a centralized metadata repository that acts as a reference point for all data assets. It eliminates the need for developers to manage siloed datasets, making it an essential tool for data discovery.

Data stores embody the repositories where data resides and could range from relational databases to cloud data warehouses and data lakes. AWS Glue can easily connect with Amazon Redshift, Amazon RDS, Amazon S3, amongst other popular databases and stores that house voluminous datasets.

ETL jobs - Extract, Transform, and Load - are the worker bees of the system. They extract data from all viable data stores, transforming inconsistencies into a consistent format, and load it into the destination database or warehouse. AWS Glue generates ETL jobs using Python or Scala, utilizing the metadata stored in the catalog. This eliminates the traditional burdens of hand-writing lines of code and manually managing jobs.

4.2. Exploring Networking Architecture

The networking architecture encompasses computing infrastructure and the configuration of virtual private clouds (VPCs), subnet groups, security groups, and endpoint policies. When correctly calibrated, these components harmonize to provide the ideal environment for the smooth flow of data.

VPCs provide an isolated section within the AWS platform where you can launch resources within a virtual network defined by you. Configurable IP address range, subnets, route tables, and gateways present the flexibility to build an IP infrastructure mimicking an on-premise network scenario within the cloud.

Subnet groups are collections of subnets from different Availability Zones that provide high availability for data stores. They enable Glue connections to operate efficiently, yielding a seamless transfer of data.

Security groups act as a firewall on an instance level, controlling the incoming and outgoing traffic. Proper configuration is paramount to protect and safeguard user data from assorted security risks and threats.

Endpoint policies manage the rules and principles to approach AWS Glue API operations, turning out to be incredibly effective in providing fine-grained access control at a granular level.

4.3. Binding Data and Networking Architectures Together

The alliance of data and networking architectures in AWS Glue forms a powerful union that cohesively manages, organizes, and manipulates vast datasets. It establishes an environment where data can be efficiently extracted, transformed, and loaded into destination databases, all within a secure and high availability network sphere.

AWS Glue's unique networking setup and a structured perspective simplify data interactions and enhance database management capabilities. Understanding and optimizing these architectural principles are pivotal to addressing common challenges that users might face, like timeout errors.

These two architectural domains don't work in isolated silos but complement one another to provide an efficient data pipeline. The degree to which you can optimize and manage these structures often determines the success of your data management and processing activities.

Conclusively, an in-depth scrutiny of data and networking architectures illuminates the intricacies of AWS Glue's functionality. With this foundational framework now understood, we can delve into more focused subjects, shedding light on how to effectively address and prevent timeout errors. Remember, it's not the system that's inherently complicated; it's our understanding that initially lacks depth. With patient exploration and the apt application of knowledge, we can transform these seemingly complex constructs into manageable components.

Chapter 5. Timeout Errors: In-depth Analysis and Explanation

The key to comprehending AWS Glue and its primary issues, such as Timeout errors, lies in first understanding the service's nature and working principle at a deeper level. So, let's begin by covering a brief overview of AWS Glue.

AWS Glue is an entirely managed extract, transform, and load (ETL) service that makes it easy for users to prepare and load their data for analytics. By providing these capabilities, AWS Glue enables businesses to analyze their data in other AWS services effortlessly, and on-premises databases.

In AWS Glue, the standard job timeout is 48 hours. However, the job might time out before 48 hours if it does not meet some conditions. AWS provides the option to increase or decrease this timeframe based on specific requirements. That said, timeout errors with AWS Glue are a common phenomenon, often leaving numerous data engineers baffled.

5.1. Understanding AWS Glue Timeout Errors

AWS Glue timeout errors often occur when the operation requested by a user on the data catalog exceeds a certain set duration, causing the AWS Glue to automatically halt the operation. The challenge here primarily stems from understanding the underlying cause that triggers such timeouts.

When the ETL job in AWS Glue fails to finish within the default timeout duration—typically 48 hours for Scala and Python shell jobs, 360 minutes for Spark jobs and five minutes for Python scripts in crawler code—the timeout error occurs. This default setting might superficially seem like the obvious cause of timeout errors. However, the real reasons can be multifaceted, varying from job design issues, data volume issues, to system resource issues, such as CPU and memory allocation.

5.2. Navigating Through Job Design Issues

Job design is a critical factor determining the performance of an ETL job. Poorly designed jobs can run for a longer duration, causing timeouts. Here are some common job design issues leading to timeouts:

1. **Lack of Parallelism**: AWS Glue is designed to leverage maximum parallelism while processing data, but this isn't automatic. If your job isn't designed to use parallel processing, it's likely to run much longer and eventually timeout.

2. **Inefficient Use of Transformations**: AWS Glue uses `ApplyMapping` and `ResolveChoice` transformations for transforming the input data. However, the transformations used might not always be the most efficient. This inefficiency often leads to substantial delays, consequently causing the job to reach the timeout limit.

3. **Dense Data Shuffle**: The `group by`, `orderBy`, and `join` clauses in AWS Glue cause data shuffles. If your data volumes are high, the shuffling operation is a heavy task, which can cause your job to timeout.

5.3. Putting Data Volume into Perspective

Another common cause of AWS Glue job timeouts is the data volume. Larger data volumes mean more batch transactions and longer runtimes, increasing the risk of timeouts. In the cases where data volume spikes unexpectedly, the task then becomes even more challenging. The job's timeout limit may need to be adjusted based on the total number of batch transactions, especially when dealing with large data sets.

For larger datasets, AWS Glue uses multiple DPUs (Data Processing Units). Adjusting the timeout limit isn't the only option available. By increasing the number of DPUs, the job can potentially process the data faster because it can handle more concurrent threads.

5.4. Managing Resource Utilization

Ignoring the management of resources such as CPU and memory leads to the inefficient functioning of AWS Glue jobs, often triggering timeout errors. The queries must be written to accommodate the capacity of the infrastructure, and the infrastructure scaled up to meet the demands of the queries.

Lack of capacity planning and managing resource utilization can also lead to such errors. When running intensive ETL jobs, pay close attention to CPU and memory usage. Using AWS CloudWatch, you can monitor these metrics. If they are consistently high, consider altering your job design or scaling your resources.

5.5. Taking Cognizance of the AWS Glue Job User Interface

The AWS Glue job user interface scrolls through log events as your job execution progresses. While this feature is beneficial, it can also lead to your browser session's timeout if your job has a large number of log events. Therefore, understanding the AWS Glue job user interface well, and handling it effectively, is pivotal to circumnavigate potential timeout errors.

5.6. Summing Up

Within AWS Glue, timeout errors constitute a widespread issue. However, understanding the structure of AWS Glue and periodically monitoring how your data flows, CPU usage, and concurrently running threads can help anticipate and avoid these errors. Although it seems like a tall order, decoding this aspect of AWS Glue will ultimately prove instrumental in optimizing ETL jobs and in getting the most out of this powerful service.

Remember, AWS Glue, as a managed service, is a complex tool that requires equally complex handling. It's a labyrinth certainly capable of leading anyone astray. Hence, think of troubleshooting methods not as one-off solutions but as an integral part of navigating this labyrinth, enhancing your overall skillset in the process.

Chapter 6. Diagnostic Techniques for Timeout Errors

A timeout error in AWS Glue job execution often signals an issue with resources, job configuration, or network connectivity. To diagnose and subsequently resolve such errors, we'll need to explore several techniques, each targeting a specific potential cause.

6.1. Understanding AWS Glue Timeout Errors

First, let's clarify what we mean by a timeout error in AWS Glue. AWS Glue Jobs, both ETL and development endpoint jobs, are governed by a maximum time that they can run uninterrupted, as defined by a parameter named `Timeout`. By default, this value is set to 2880 minutes (or 2 days). However, it can be adjusted according to your specific requirements.

If a job's execution time exceeds the specified `Timeout` value, AWS Glue throws a `TimeoutException`, halting the job execution. This error doesn't necessarily mean there's something wrong with your job's code. It might merely be that your job needs more time to complete.

6.2. Identifying the Cause of Timeout Errors

Debugging a timeout error involves identifying its root cause—whether it's due to network connectivity issues, a poorly configured job, or resource bottlenecks.

1. **Review the AWS Glue Job Logs:** By enabling logs, you can capture detailed log events for AWS Glue jobs and forward them to Amazon CloudWatch logs. Logging gives you insight into what your job is doing, where errors occur, and can reveal areas where your job may be inefficient.

> The `TimeoutException` error generally indicates that your job exceeded its maximum runtime without completing, so looking for performance-related problems might be a good starting point.

2. **Enabling AWS Glue Job Metrics:** AWS Glue Job Metrics allows you to monitor nine pre-defined metrics for your Glue jobs. These capture execution times, success rates, timeout occurrences, and more. With these, you can learn how often the timeouts occur and if there's a pattern to identify.

3. **Checking Network Connectivity:** Network connectivity can be a less obvious cause for timeout errors, especially if your AWS Glue job is attempting to connect to external data sources or APIs.

> Check your VPC network configurations and ensure adequate access to and from the necessary resources. In cases where you're trying to connect to external resources, their network settings need to be configured correctly as well.

6.3. Optimizing the AWS Glue Job Configuration

If your job takes too long to run (even when it doesn't not time out), it's likely not as efficient as it could be. Adopting the following tactics might result in noticeable performance uplift:

1. **Enable Concurrent DPUs:** By default, an AWS Glue job uses 10 DPUs. However, you can increase this number to a maximum of 100 DPUs, resulting in your job running faster. The caveat is the cost—as the number of DPUs increase, so does your bill.

2. **Increasing the Timeout Value:** If you're certain your job is functioning correctly and merely needs more time to complete, consider increasing the timeout value. However, this isn't recommended as a blanket solution. Analyze why your job is taking long, to correct inefficiencies.

3. **Activating Job Bookmarking:** AWS Glue provides a feature named "Job Bookmarking" that tracks data processed during ETL jobs, only analyzing processed data in incremental runs—ensuring jobs complete faster.

6.4. Resources and Bottleneck Analysis

If a particular job that usually runs without timing out suddenly starts experiencing timeout errors, your first check should be the processing resources.

Review your data processing pipeline end-to-end, identifying potential bottlenecks. Ensure the allocated resources match the job's requirements. For example, inadequate CPU or memory can slow your AWS Glue job, leading to timeout errors.

6.5. Conclusion

AWS Glue is a mighty cog in the AWS data processing machinery but it's not without its quirks. As data amounts handled by businesses continue to grow, AWS Glue's role will likely become even more significant.

Mastering the art of diagnosing and resolving AWS Glue timeout errors will prove a valuable skill. Remember—patience and thoroughness are vital attributes while troubleshooting. Take time to understand your problems and address them systematically—your prize will be the well-oiled, smoothly running AWS Glue jobs upon which your business relies.

Chapter 7. Real-world Case Studies of Timeout Errors

AWS Glue has established itself as a leading ETL (Extract, Transform, Load) service that simplifies and automates the heavy lifting of data preparation. However, like all sophisticated software, it's not immune to problems—one of the most frequent being timeout errors. As we delve into a comprehensive exploration of this prevalent issue, we will examine real-world case studies, deriving a wealth of knowledge from these practical instances.

7.1. Case Study 1: Timeout Error during Glue Job Execution

In our first case, a user reported that while executing a Glue job to transform and load data into Amazon Redshift, they faced timeout errors. Upon inspection, the Glue logs revealed that the job was timing out during the connection establishment to Redshift.

After evaluating the scenario, it was discovered that an increase in the data volume had led to timeouts. The solution to the issue was two-fold:

1. The instance type for AWS Glue was upgraded to a more powerful configuration. A stronger instance ensures better handling of larger data volumes.

2. The user was advised to optimize their data partitioning, spreading it across multiple data processing units (DPUs). Better partitioning ensures faster, more efficient processing.

7.2. Case Study 2: Timeout Error in Triggering Glue Jobs

Another common scenario surfaced when a user was scheduling a set of Glue jobs to be triggered sequentially. The user reported that sometimes, the dependent jobs wouldn't start at all after the preceding job completed, throwing a timeout error.

Upon scrutiny, the under-optimization of the provisioning of concurrency resources turned out to be the culprit. The AWS Glue scheduler uses this provision to run and manage jobs concurrently.

To rectify this:

1. The AWS Glue resource quotas were increased considering the user's demand for higher concurrency.

2. The user was further advised to structure their job workflows better by using AWS Glue triggers, creating a defined dependency between jobs.

7.3. Case Study 3: Timeout Errors due to Network Issues

In this case, the AWS Glue job failed with a timeout error, and after studying the logs, the faults pointed to network latency issues. It became evident that the user's AWS Glue job was trying to connect to an external data source outside of the VPC (Virtual Private Cloud), leading to network connection timeouts.

The remedial measures undertaken were:

1. Setting up VPC endpoints to ensure secure, direct, and reliable network connectivity between the AWS Glue job and the external data source.

2. Enabling Glue job retries and increasing the timeout value, making it more tolerant to occasional network latencies.

7.4. Case Study 4: Timeout Errors in AWS Glue Crawlers

Timeout errors aren't exclusive to Glue jobs-- they also affect Glue crawlers. This was evident when a user reported their Glue crawler timing out while attempting to catalog a large amount of data.

The issue was traced back to inappropriate data partitioning with a large number of individual files in an S3 bucket. Handling these as a single bulk load led to timeout errors.

The resolution path included:

1. Optimizing data partitioning and reducing the file count by aggregating smaller files.

2. Increasing the timeout value for the Glue crawler allowing it to allocate more time to catalog the data.

Through these case studies, we've seen how timeout errors in AWS Glue can manifest in various scenarios and how they can be practically addressed. While the solutions to these problems were specific, the broader lesson we should draw is that error-free data processing requires a carefully optimized and provisioned environment. AWS Glue is a robust and flexible tool, but its performance is often dependent on how well other parts of the AWS environment are set up to handle data, how the data is partitioned, and how the instance types are chosen depending on the volume of the data.

Care and attention to these elements will pre-emptively solve many timeout-related issues, making for a smoother, more efficient data processing workflow.

Such proactive strategies not only fix existing problems but also future-proof your data operations, making you adept at avoiding similar issues down the line and giving you a critical edge in the exciting and growing field of cloud computing and big data processing.

Chapter 8. Mitigation Strategies for Timeout Errors

In the ongoing troubleshooting saga with AWS Glue timeout errors, a well-crafted mitigation strategy marks the first significant step towards resolution. As you navigate this expanse, understanding potential causes of these errors is critical to developing effective troubleshooting solutions.

8.1. Understanding Timeout Errors

Timeout errors in AWS Glue can occur due to various reasons: from simple network connection issues to more complex problems like resource-intensive ETL jobs resulting in a failure to retrieve data within the allocated time. Understanding these causes can provide valuable insights into devising effective mitigation strategies.

8.1.1. Network Connection Issues

Many timeout errors are caused by challenges in network connectivity. The server might not respond in time due to traffic congestion, physical network interruptions, or the instability of your ISP's infrastructure. To mitigate such issues, consider configuring automatic retries in your code or increasing timeout parameters within acceptable limits. Be careful not to stretch these parameters too far, as it could hide underlying problems.

8.1.2. Resource-intensive ETL Jobs

When your AWS Glue ETL jobs are heavily resource-intensive, they may cause timeout errors. Such jobs often involve processing vast amounts of data or using demanding processing techniques. Monitoring and optimizing the resources your ETL jobs consume can significantly reduce the occurrence of these errors.

8.2. Categorizing Timeout Errors

Categorizing timeout errors based on their frequency and impact can streamline mapping out the strategic measures against them and tailor these strategies to unique situations.

8.2.1. Occasional Errors

If timeout errors occur sporadically, indirect factors like transient network issues or temporary AWS outages might be the culprits. These errors can typically be resolved through automatic retries.

8.2.2. Recurring Errors

When timeout errors are chronic, they often hint at systematic problems. These might include improperly configured settings or resource-heavy ETL jobs. For such troubles, a deep-dive investigation is necessary—regular monitoring, careful log analysis, and refactoring your ETL scripts might be in order.

8.3. Automatic Retry Configuration

An automatic retry mechanism is one of the primary measures against timeout errors that occur due to transient network issues or temporary AWS outages. It provides your ETL jobs another chance to execute the failed operation without user intervention.

To configure automatic retries, you will need to alter your ETL script slightly. Here's a code snippet that uses Python's boto3 library:

```python
import boto3
from botocore.config import Config
```

```python
config = Config(retries={"max_attempts": 10, "mode":
"standard"})
client = boto3.client("glue", config=config)
```

This snippet will configure the script to retry a failed operation a maximum of 10 times before finally giving up and throwing a timeout error.

8.4. Optimizing Job Resources

Optimizing the resources used by your ETL jobs is an essential strategy to counteract timeout errors caused by resource-intensive processes.

8.4.1. Tuning Memory and CPU Allocation

AWS Glue allows you to manage the memory and CPU allocation of your ETL jobs. By increasing these resources, you can ensure your scripts run more efficiently, reducing the chances of a timeout error.

But remember, increasing resources isn't always the solution. It's imperative to ensure that your ETL job is using resources efficiently. Excessive memory or CPU allocation can lead to wasted resources and increased AWS costs.

8.4.2. Partitioning Your Data

Data partitioning is a proven strategy in the world of big data processing. By breaking up your dataset into more manageable chunks, you enable parallel processing, reducing the total time it takes to complete your ETL jobs.

The key to successful partitioning is understanding your data. Factors such as data distribution, size, and data access patterns all play a role in deciding how best to partition your data.

In conclusion, timeout errors with AWS Glue, while challenging, are not insurmountable. By understanding these errors and implementing thoughtful mitigation strategies, you can alleviate the impact these issues have on your ETL operations. This journey may be intricate, but it's rewarding—the deeper you delve into these issues, the more proficient you'll become in navigating the vast realms of AWS Glue and cloud data processing.

Chapter 9. Innovative Tools and Techniques to Combat Timeout Errors

Before we dive into the manifold strategies, tools, and techniques employed to combat, diagnose, and prevent AWS Glue Timeout errors, it is essential to set the stage with a solid understanding of what Timeout errors are. A Timeout error occurs when a request—made to a server or a database, for example—takes longer to process than the predetermined threshold. In the context of AWS Glue, these issues primarily occur during ETL (Extract, Transform, Load) jobs, crawlers, or development endpoints, especially when these jobs handle voluminous and complex data workloads.

9.1. The AWS Glue Environment

The AWS Glue environment consists of various elements that each play a crucial role in carrying out Big Data solutions competently. It involves AWS Glue Studio, ETL Jobs, Data Catalog, Crawlers, Development Endpoints, and more. Timeout errors within this environment can be a result of numerous predicaments; exhaustive load on servers, unoptimized queries, network issues, or even poorly configured system settings, to name a few.

9.2. Employing AWS Glue Job Monitoring

The first line of defense against Timeout errors is effectual monitoring, providing invaluable diagnostic information. AWS Glue offers a few inbuilt monitoring tools:

- AWS Glue Console - It provides an overview of job runs, their status, and a brief report on any error encountered.

- AWS CloudWatch - Provides more detailed metrics, such as 'Job Success Rate', 'Job Timeout', 'Mapping Choices Selected', and 'Seconds to Complete', among others. For our purpose, the 'Job Timeout' metric is particularly pertinent.

AWS CloudWatch deserves an expanded exploration. This service provides the option to set alarms for various thresholds, an excellent preventive mechanism against potential timeout situations. For instance, you can configure an alarm to notify you when a job exceeds its average execution time. Detailed instructions on setting up CloudWatch alarms can be found on the official AWS documentation.

The Amazon CloudWatch Logs Insights service is also an indispensable resource, enabling you to interactively search, filter, and analyze log data from AWS CloudWatch Logs. This service makes it easier to glean information about any discrepancies, including Timeout errors.

9.3. Optimization of AWS Glue Jobs

The next pivotal countenance in our expedition is optimizing AWS Glue jobs to help prevent Timeout errors. Following are some of the essential techniques:

- ETL job tuning - Fine-tuning parameters like 'MaxCapacity' and 'Timeout' could significantly impact job performance. MaxCapacity indicates the maxim number of data processing units(Glue DPUs) that can be allocated to this job, and Timeout indicates the time after which a job is forcibly terminated. AWS provides specific guidelines to tune these parameters based on job requirements.

- Correct Schema Selection - AWS Glue utilizes a dynamic schema approach, meaning the schema isn't set rigidly, and there could be slight changes in how fields map during ETL execution. This flexibility can cause timeouts in complex jobs. Explicitly stating the schema provides stability and helps negate the likelihood of timeouts.

- Programming language choice - AWS Glue currently supports Spark scripts written in Python and Scala. These languages have different characteristics that can impact job performance. Opting for an appropriate language based on the job nature might mitigate timeout issues.

9.4. SQL Performance Tuning

SQL forms the backbone of query operations in Big Data ETL processes. Significant optimization can be achieved by refining SQL commands, potentially curtailing timeout errors. A few useful tactics involve:

- Utilization of Apache Arrow for high-speed, in-memory data transfer.

- Reduction of Data Shuffling, a process that may cause a significant delay in task execution.

- Avoiding large JOIN operations where possible to save on compute resources.

9.5. Alternative Tools

Finally, it's crucial to be aware that AWS Glue does not function in isolation. Helpful integrations, such as AWS Glue DataBrew for data preparation tasks, or Athena for ad-hoc querying, can spread the workload burden, thus reducing the occurrence of timeouts.

While AWS Glue is an effective data storage and ETL service, encountering Timeout errors can yield a fair amount of frustration.

However, the wide-ranging toolset at hand—from CloudWatch logs for diagnostic monitoring, tuning ETL jobs to optimal performance strategies, utilizing other AWS services, and improving SQL performance—can help alleviate these issues, fortified with appropriate precautionary measures.

Naturally, innovation is inherent to technology's progression. It is vital to stay agile, durable, and consistently attentive to updates and new techniques to ensure the smooth operation of AWS Glue Jobs and to maintain their resilience against Timeout errors. By assimilating these strategies into your process and understandings, you should feel more armed to tackle the potential issues that come with the dynamic world of AWS Glue. Remember that, in the end, understanding and addressing a problem is just as important as preventing one.

Chapter 10. Best Practices to Prevent AWS Glue Timeout Errors

AWS Glue, a fully managed extract, transform, and load (ETL) service, makes it easy to prepare and load your data for analytics. It can analyze (or "crawl") your data, deduce a schema, and generate ETL code in Python or Scala to move, transform, and clean your data. However, as with any tool, errors can occur occasionally. One of these dreaded errors is the notorious AWS Glue Timeout Error.

10.1. Understanding Timeout Errors

Before diving into best practices to prevent timeout errors, we must first gain insight into what these errors are and why they can occur. AWS Glue Timeout Errors usually mean that a particular operation took longer than the configured or allowed job execution time.

These errors can be divided into two major categories: . Job-timeout: The job docs not finish within the maximum timeout limit. The timeout limit is configurable and can range from 5 minutes to 48 hours. . Resource-timeout: This is related to individual resources that your ETL job uses and may vary depending on the underlying resource.

10.2. Proper Management of AWS Glue Jobs

To prevent AWS Glue job timeouts, one needs to closely monitor job performance, manage resources wisely, and modify job timeouts appropriately.

Understand your data: AWS Glue derives a schema for your dataset and generates mechanisms to transform and load your data. If your data is diverse and varies greatly, automatic schema derivation might face difficulty and can thus cause delays. It's crucial to know your data and provide an explicit schema where needed, which will save compute resources and time.

Job Monitoring: Monitoring AWS Glue job metrics using AWS CloudWatch can give you actionable insights about a job's performance and runtime characteristics. This can help you identify problematic job stages and the causes of timeouts.

Manage resources wisely: All AWS Glue jobs use certain resources, like a Data Catalog, connections, crawlers, endpoints, job bookmarks and the likes. Given the nature of Timeout Errors, it is apparent that an unnecessary long use of these resources can lead to such errors. So, it's important to ensure that these resources are appropriately used.

Modify timeout limits: If everything else fails and your job still does not run within the set boundary, you might have to tweak the 'Timeout property'. The maximum limit is 48 hours, so make sure the set limit is appropriate depending on the job's capacity and requirements.

10.3. Utilizing AWS Glue Job Bookmarks

AWS Glue job bookmarks help maintain state information and ensure the reliability of ETL jobs. This feature enables Glue to keep track of data that has already been processed during previous runs of an ETL job, thus avoiding reprocessing of the data.

To use bookmarks effectively, make sure to enable them during the initial run of your job. You can activate job bookmarks by setting the jobBookmark option to one of the following: . job-bookmark-enable: Commits bookmarks and removes previously-committed ones. . job-bookmark-pause: Commits no new bookmarks but uses previously committed ones. . job-bookmark-disable: Ignores all bookmarks.

10.4. Leveraging AWS Glue Data Catalog

AWS Glue Data Catalog is a fully managed, Apache Hive Metastore compatible, metadata repository. This catalog maintains a unified view of all your data across various data stores.

Consistent use of Data Catalog can significantly reduce potential points of failure. The catalog is responsible for storing and retrieving table metadata.

10.5. AWS Glue Version Impact

Different AWS Glue versions can also influence the occurrence of timeout errors. Advanced Glue versions offer enhanced performance and should be used when feasible. With each new release, Gluc becomes more refined and efficient, enabling it to handle bigger datasets more rapidly, and thereby reducing the chances of timeout errors.

10.6. AWS Glue Error Handling Techniques

Error handling is a crucial step in the creation of successful and fault-tolerant ETL workflows. AWS Glue supports a variety of error handling mechanisms like Try-catch blocks and Job bookmarks.

When creating python shell jobs, you can execute error handling using the Python try-except block. Python shell jobs are for custom scripts that coordinate other Glue jobs, extracting complex relationships or moving to another data store, which don't follow an Apache Spark execution model.

10.7. Conclusion

Preventing AWS Glue Timeout Errors requires a profound understanding of the micro-service itself, as well as related services like CloudWatch, Data Catalog, and others. It's a constant cycle of learning, troubleshooting, optimizing, and learning again. A journey of growth in the intriguing world of Big-data processing, transforming the most annoying problem into a chance to learn more and do better. Remember, the cloud is the limit!

Chapter 11. Developing Robust and Efficient Data pipelines with AWS Glue

Developing robust and efficient data pipelines with AWS Glue starts with understanding the key ingredients of this platform — Crawlers, Jobs, and Scheduling processes. These form the core elements that contribute to the power of AWS Glue in automated data processing.

11.1. Understanding Crawlers, Jobs, and Scheduling

A crawler in AWS Glue connects to the source where your data is stored — such as Amazon S3, Amazon RDS, or other databases running on AWS. It then scans the data in the source to generate metadata tables, which are stored in the Glue Data Catalog. Any changes made in the data source can be translated and tracked in the Data Catalog through the crawler. Understanding how to set up and manage these crawlers is key in making the most out of AWS Glue.

The job in AWS Glue is where ETL (Extract, Transform, Load) operations occur. AWS Glue generates Python or Scala code for your ETL process. You can either use the proposed code or modify it as per your needs. Efficient handling of these jobs contributes significantly to avoiding timeout errors.

Scheduling in AWS Glue helps automate your ETL jobs. Defining schedules for data movement or transformation allows you to avoid congestion during peak times, thereby reducing the likelihood of timeout errors.

11.2. Mastering AWS Glue Crawlers

Crawlers play a pivotal role in gathering data from multiple sources in AWS. Here are step by step instructions to grasp crawler functionalities:

1. Navigate to the AWS Glue Console and select 'Crawlers' on the left sidebar menu.

2. Click 'Add crawler' to initiate a new one.

3. Add a name, description (optional), and continue to the next page.

4. Specify the data store and path. Continue.

5. Add another data store if needed. Otherwise, just continue.

6. Choose an IAM role that gives AWS Glue permission to access your data store or create a new one by following instructions.

7. In the Frequency field, specify when the crawler should run. For a one-time run, choose 'On demand'.

8. Configure the output to your database and prefix for your tables (optional).

9. Review and finish the process.

11.3. Optimizing AWS Glue Jobs

Below are some essential tips to optimize the efficiency of an AWS Glue job:

- Understand and Adjust the Resources Used for Your Job: AWS Glue uses DPUs (Data Processing Units) for processing and executing jobs. The more DPUs you allocate, the more resources AWS Glue has to run your job, increasing its speed. However, while it may be tempting to increase DPUs as much as possible, learning to adjust resources appropriately can save costs and avoid overloading the system, which might result in a timeout error.

- Tune Your SQL Operations: AWS Glue uses Apache Spark behind the scenes, and one of the most common causes of slow job performance and timeouts is poorly optimized SQL queries. Consider using Spark SQL's higher-order functions that perform calculations on arrays or map datatypes. Practices such as reducing shuffling of data across partitions, avoiding operations that require data movement, and minimizing the use of user-defined functions (UDFs) can significantly speed up the run time and avoid timeouts.

- Handle Late-Arriving Data: AWS Glue jobs can also time out if there are issues with late-arriving data. Architect your pipeline to handle this situation effectively by maintaining a staging area for late-arriving data.

11.4. Streamlining AWS Glue Scheduling

Automation helps you run ETL jobs per a pre-defined schedule. Here's how you can set this up:

1. From your AWS Glue console, navigate to Jobs.

2. Select the job you want to schedule.

3. In the Job properties section, under Job run settings, select 'Edit job' to modify it.

4. Under 'Maximum capacity', determine the amount of capacity you need for this job to run.

5. Determine a frequency at which to initiate job runs.

6. Specify a time at which the scheduled job should start.

7. Click on 'Finish and Save'.

In conclusion, developing robust and efficient data pipelines with AWS Glue involves understanding how crawlers, jobs, and scheduling processes interconnect. The more proficient you become in handling these elements, the less you'll grapple with the notorious issue of timeout errors. Thus, AWS Glue becomes a powerful tool for your big data processing tasks.